What a Mess!

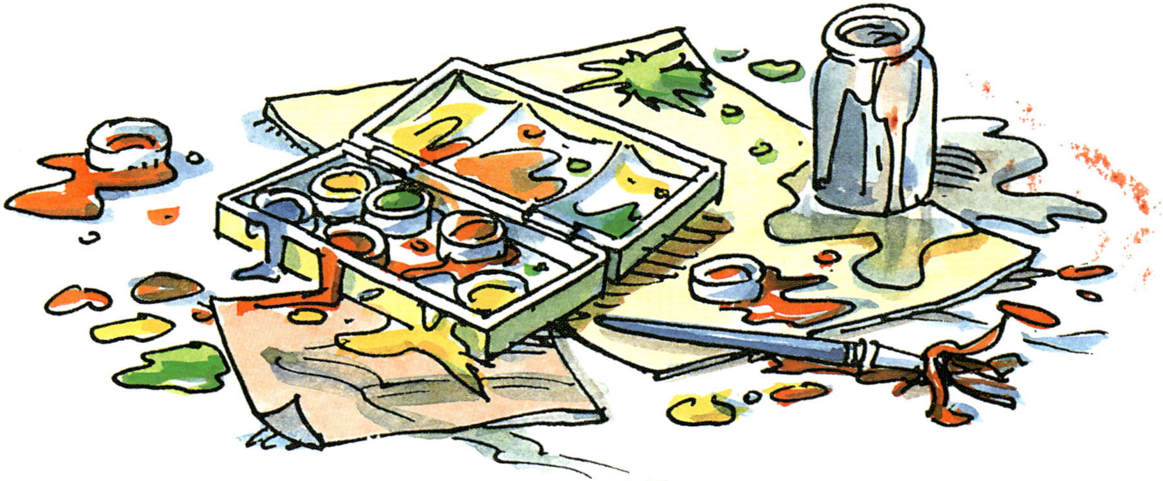

Story by Tony Mitton
Illustrations by Philippe Dupasquier

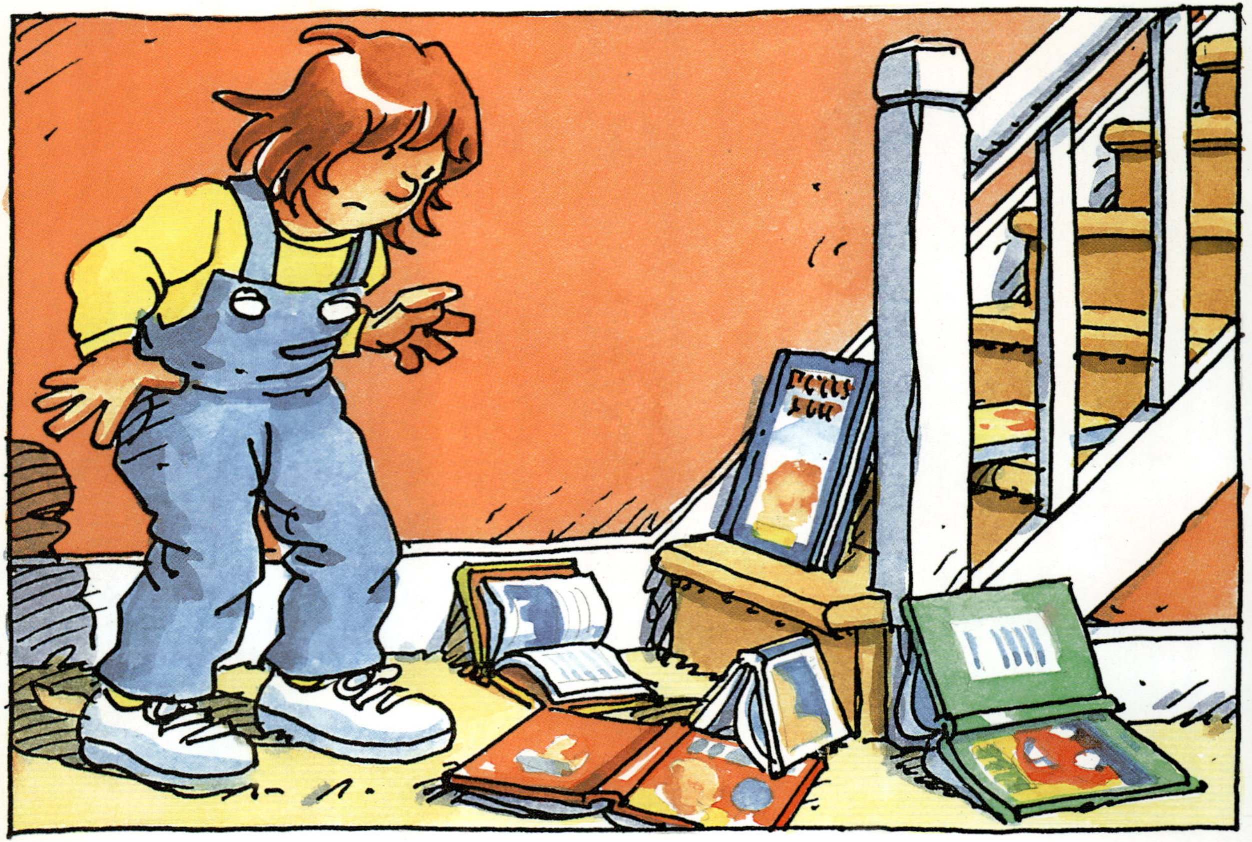

My books!

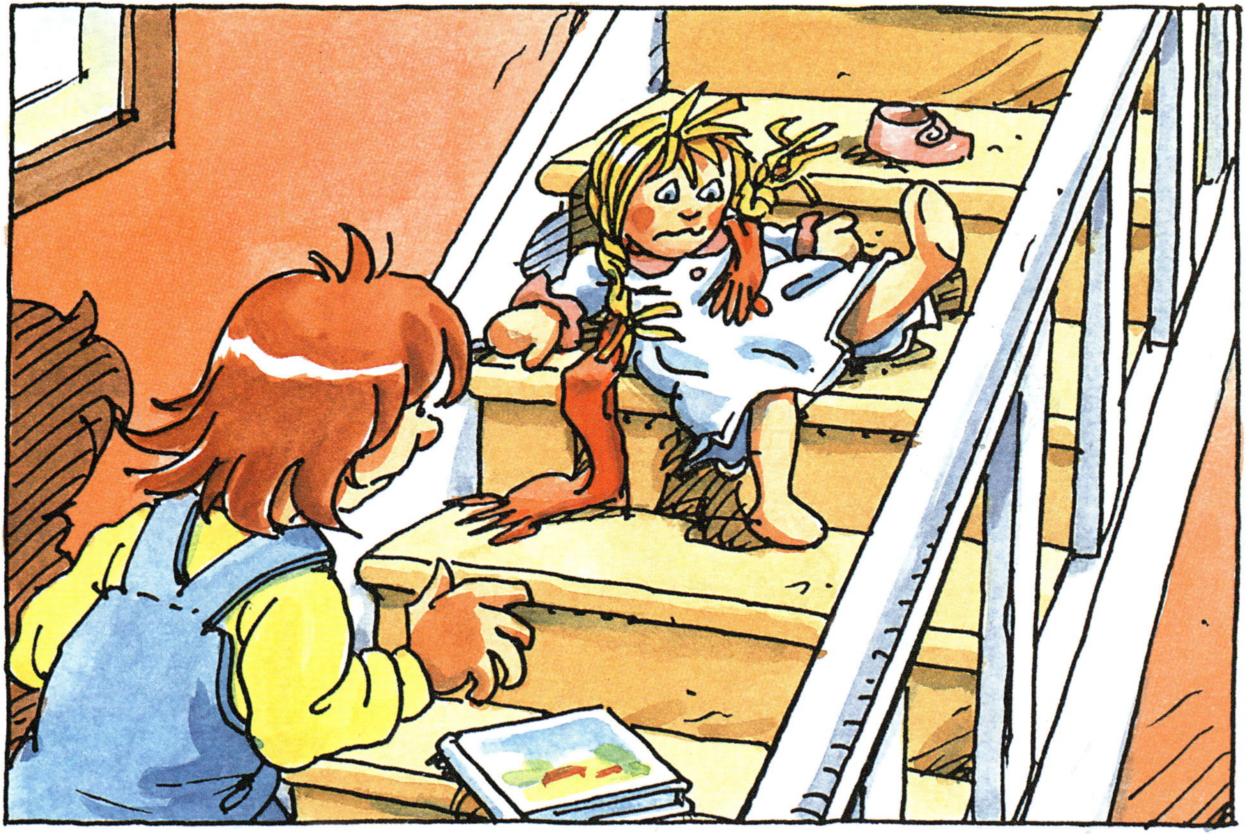

My doll!

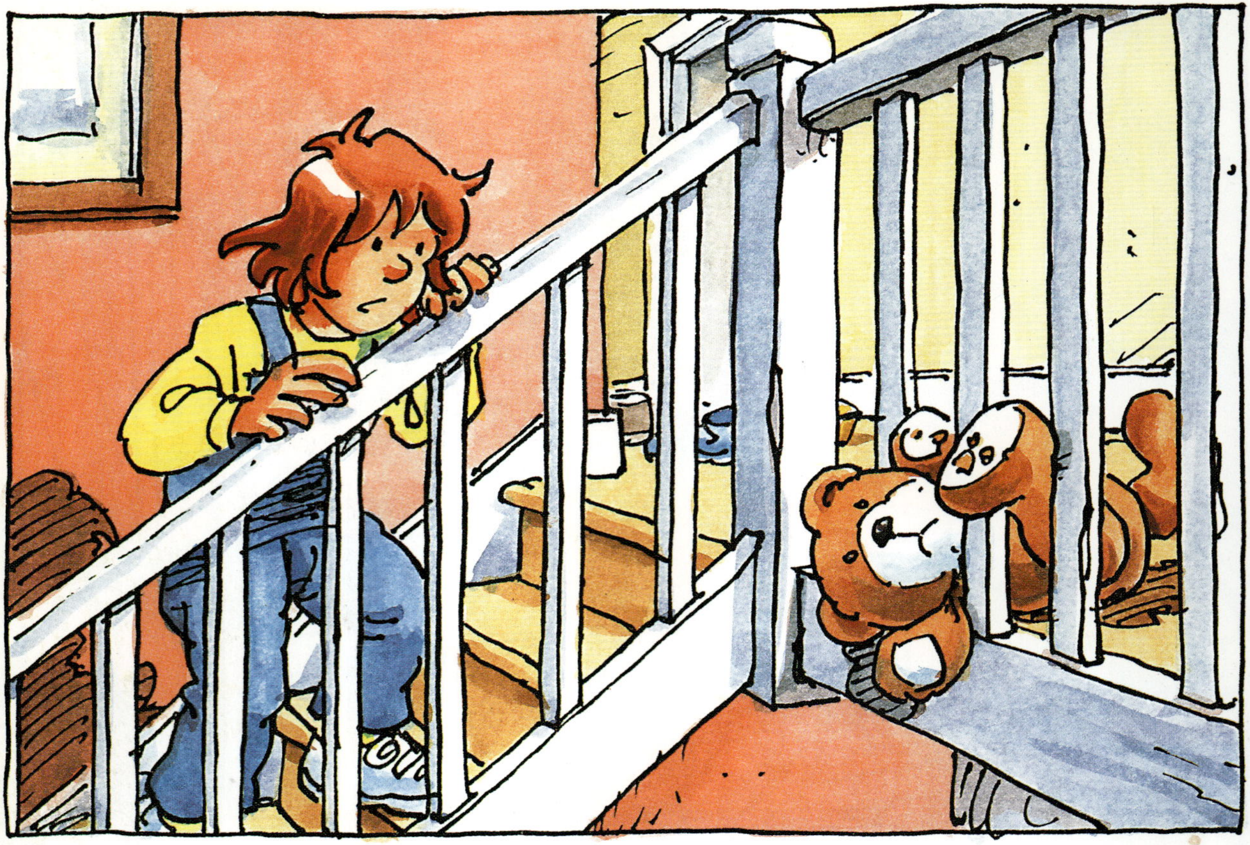

My teddy!

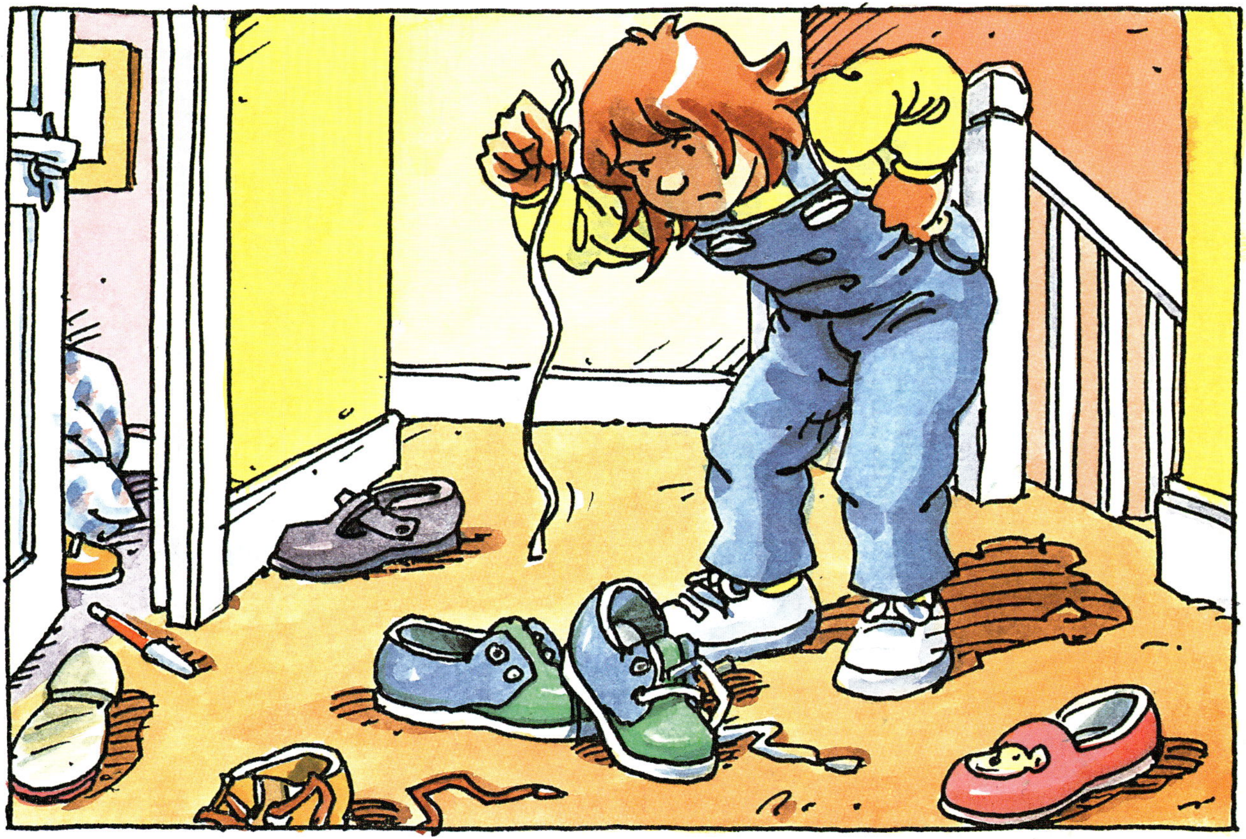

My shoes!

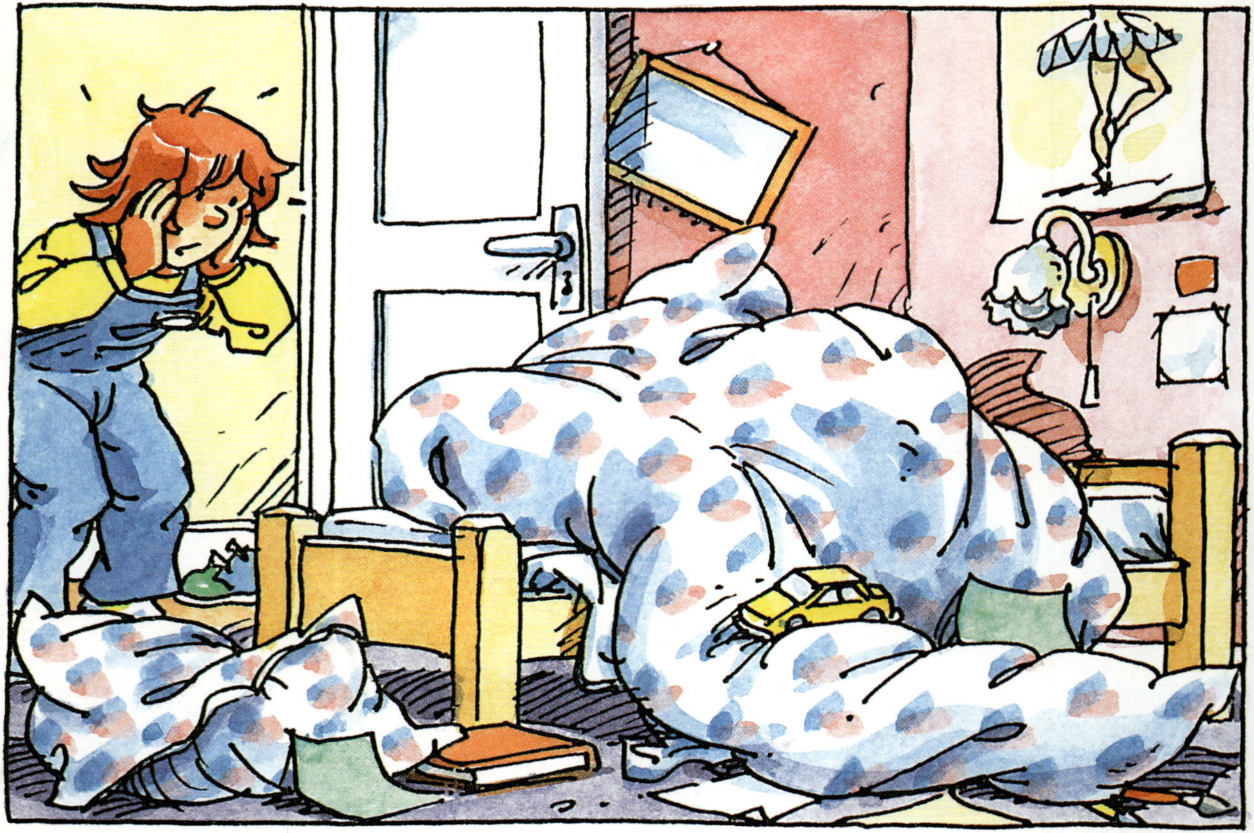

My bed!

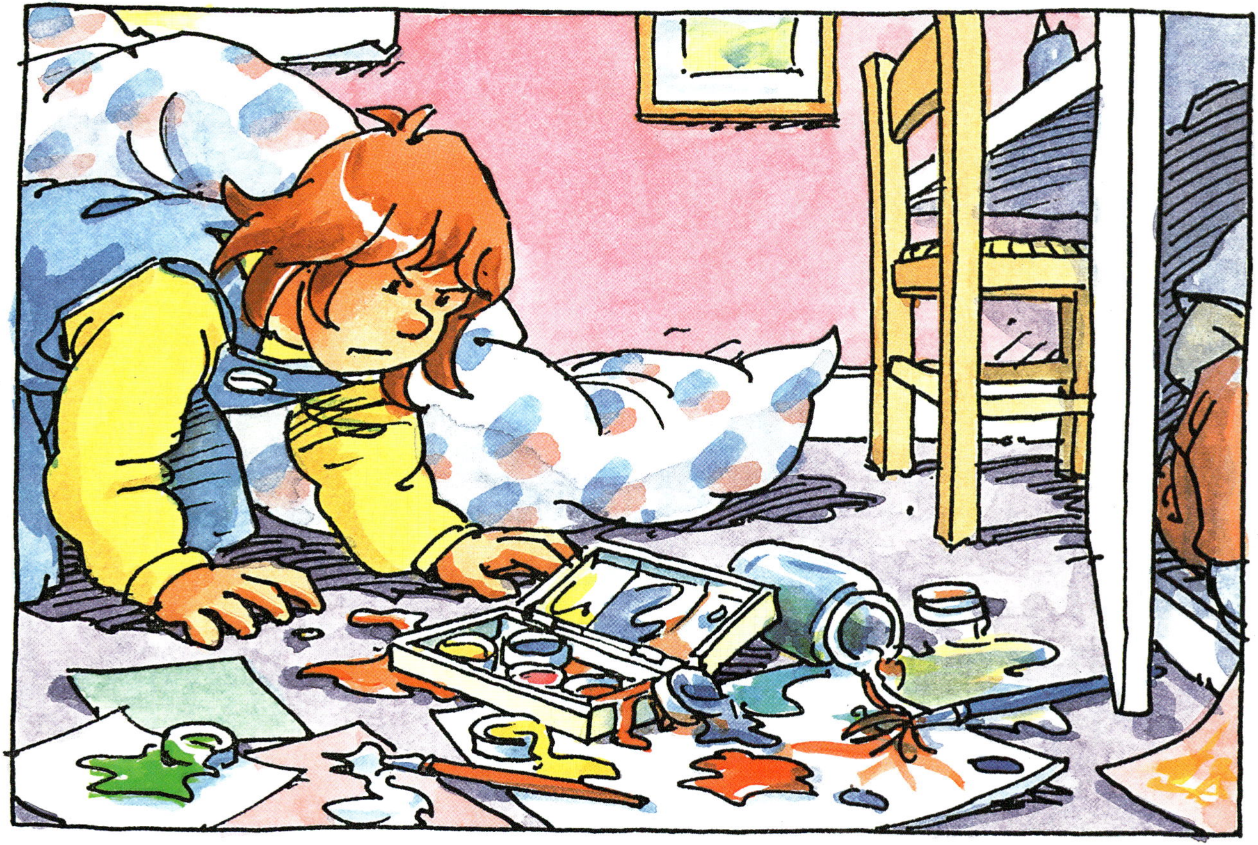

My paints!

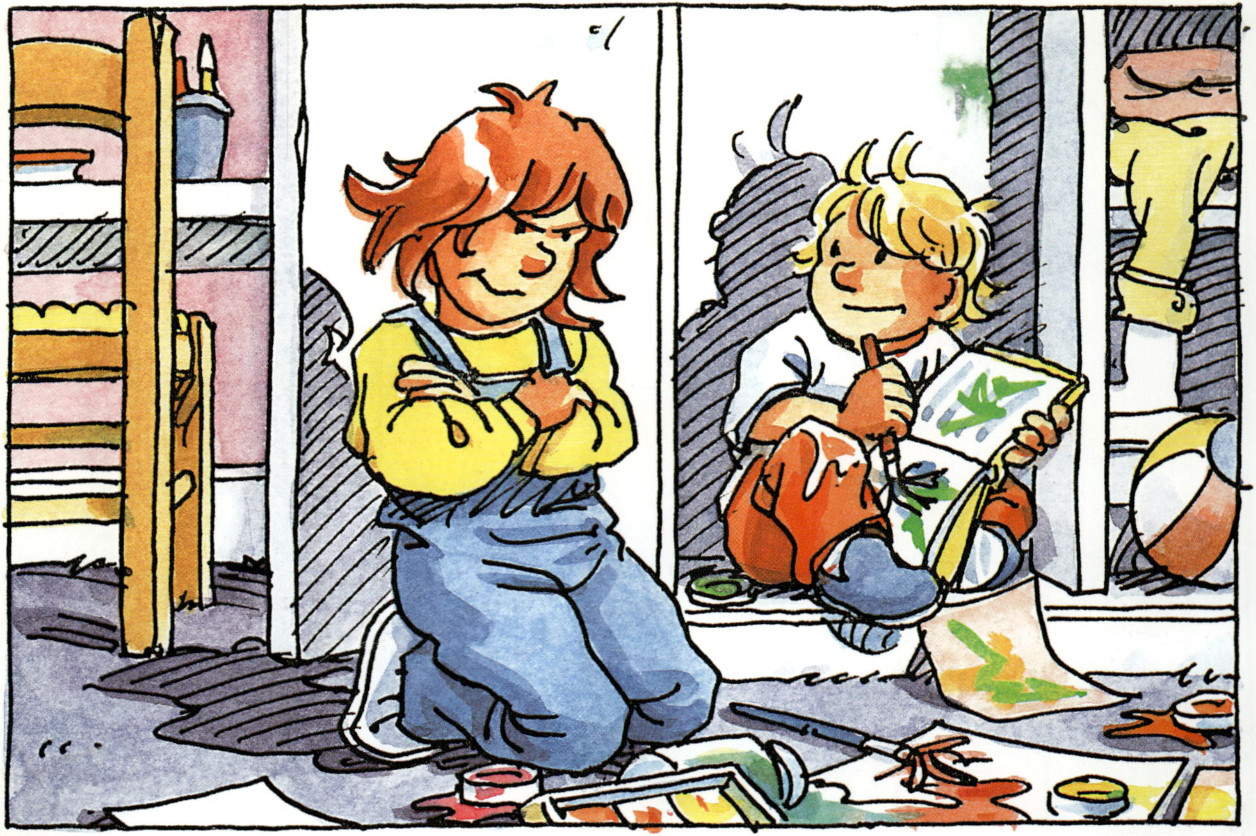

My brother!